BOOK OF True Life POEMS

Dave Courtney-Shore

I dedicate this book, firstly, to my family and friends...

With thanks for all the adventures along life's journey
Where I eventually found myself and my soul.

The book is also a dedication to life......

In all its phases from birth to death,
witnessing all the hopes and joys, pitfalls and disasters
that befall us along the way.

ISBN: 978-1-64314-694-2 (Paperback)
978-1-64314-695-9 (Hardback)
978-1-64314-696-6 (E-book)

AUTHORS PRESS

AuthorsPress
California, USA
www.authorspress.com

Contents

The Journey of Life

Birth—A New Beginning

Everyone is singing
A new life–a new beginning
A new member of the family
This little bundle of happiness and joy
Is it a girl or is it a boy?

Who cares?
Overwhelming, miraculous, stupendous
Bring it on
Oh no, twins

Oh dear, here comes another one!

Childhood

An adventure every day
Something new, magical, mysterious
In every new wonderful way.

Wondrous stories
Wondrous times
A smile on my face
Having fun
Whenever I can
Wherever I run.

Learning, listening, copying, coping
Moving forward cautiously
Each stumble taken
One tumble at a time.

Like a beat of a drum
Waking, walking, listening, learning,
Walking, talking, playing, gaming
Feeding, sleeping
Boy it's exhausting
Don't believe me
You should see my Mum!

All in one day
Boy it's so much fun
Let it be forever
Let it rock on!

Yet sometimes rebelling,
Getting into trouble
Must be done.
Until caught
Nowhere to hide
Nowhere to run.

Told to stop!
Told to behave
Tried to complain
Put in my playpen
Dummy in mouth
To shut me up
And told to play.

Occasional Pain
A fall, a strain
Bang my head
As I fall off the bed
Try to remember
Don't do that again.

A finger burnt against a radiator that's hot
Water in the bath, burning my bot
Sun on my face, cheeks burnt and red
Is Mom looking after me
Feels like she's not.

So what?
A splash here, splash there
Water over the bath
Spreading over the floor
Going everywhere.

Let it run
So much fun!
Game on.

Children of Destiny

They are Strong
They are Thoughtful
Resourceful
Resolute and Sound.

Winning
Overcoming All
It's their Duty
For this they are Bound.

And whilst I am a Survivor
They are Warriors
With Swords raised High
Cutting away the Rot and Dross
That blocks their Way
As they march Onward
Dispensing Justice
Routinely
Every Day.

Living the Dream
Leaving Nothing Behind
Moving Swiftly On
Being Bold
Remaining Strong.

Soldiers of Faith not Fortune
Bold, Honest and True
With Banners Flying Aloft
Striding Forward
Always Forthright
Taking the High Ground
Taking in the View.

With Purpose and Conviction
Holders of Hope
Honesty and Virtue
For which they are Proud
For that which they have Fought
And truly Found.

Blessed with Morals
Different from Others
They stand out in a Crowd
It's not that they are necessarily
Handsome or Beautiful
Not that they Boast or are Loud
But they are Steadfast
Standing Firm and Proud
Standing out amongst Others
Far away from the Tricks and Taunts
Of the baying Madding Crowd.

Sometimes Distant and Alone
Sometimes sitting on their Throne
Masters of their Destiny
Life in their Hands
Life with Meaning
Life without Bounds.

Each Child Different
In their own Special Way
Each has the Look
But nothing you see in a Glossy Magazine
Or read from a Library Book.

Yes, People look up to Them
Some with Respect
Some with Jealousy
Some Forlorn
Some Downtrodden
Some with Scorn.

But they just Stand There
Sound of Mind
Body Sturdy and Strong
Taking on Anything
They Find.

Choosing Right from Wrong
Mortal, Immortal
It doesn't Matter
For the Meaning of Life
They have truly Found.

They know the way
They know who they are
Where they belong
What they will find
Leaving nothing untouched
Leaving nothing and no-one behind.

Sons

So much to be cherished with heart-felt thanks
To see a son grow up with his Father close at hand
And the warmth and love of his Mother
Watching on as they play.

Sometimes strict, sometimes over the top
Sometimes overly protective, sometimes not
A Father's role difficult at times
To see his son do better
And do what his father did
but should not.

And as for his Mother
Always proud and true
Always thinking the best
Of him and what he can do.

As for the Son
Much to learn
Much to bear on one's shoulders
As they grow and turn
Into muscle and manhood
Independence and might
As they venture into the world to earn
their way
And meet their plight.

Daughters

Born from God
Heavenly in every way
Pure and innocent like the dawning of a new day
They grow into a Princess everyone wants to know
Sincere and honest like the driven snow.

Blessed with grace
Cares and carrying the World in their embrace
Their love shines with an ambiance and with no disgrace.

Like an Angel from up high
True light, love divine
Yet feet on earth
Solid like the ground
They walk on
With destiny to be appreciated
And duty bound.

With purity of soul
No-one can deny
No-one like them
They will not fail.

Yes heaven sent
Blessed and pure
Love and kindness
Abounds and spreads before them
Yes, you can see and feel it
In the very depths of their souls.

Yes God has blessed us
Let it touch our hearts
Let it last forever
And keep us together
Never apart.

Tribute to a Chinese Prodigy

Like Fan Bing Bing, you can act model and sing
You could be a leading actress, like Vicky Chen
You play the piano like the virtuoso, Yang Yang
You have a sweet voice and a cute smile, like Teresa Teng.

You can pirouette and fly through the air like Rudolph Nureyev
Always smiling, laughing, dancing and play acting.
Are you Shirley Temple,
Fred Astaire
or Charlie Chaplin?

You can be them all
And undoubtedly with all the charms
of Princess Grace,

Above all else
You are a little Princess.

Being a Teen

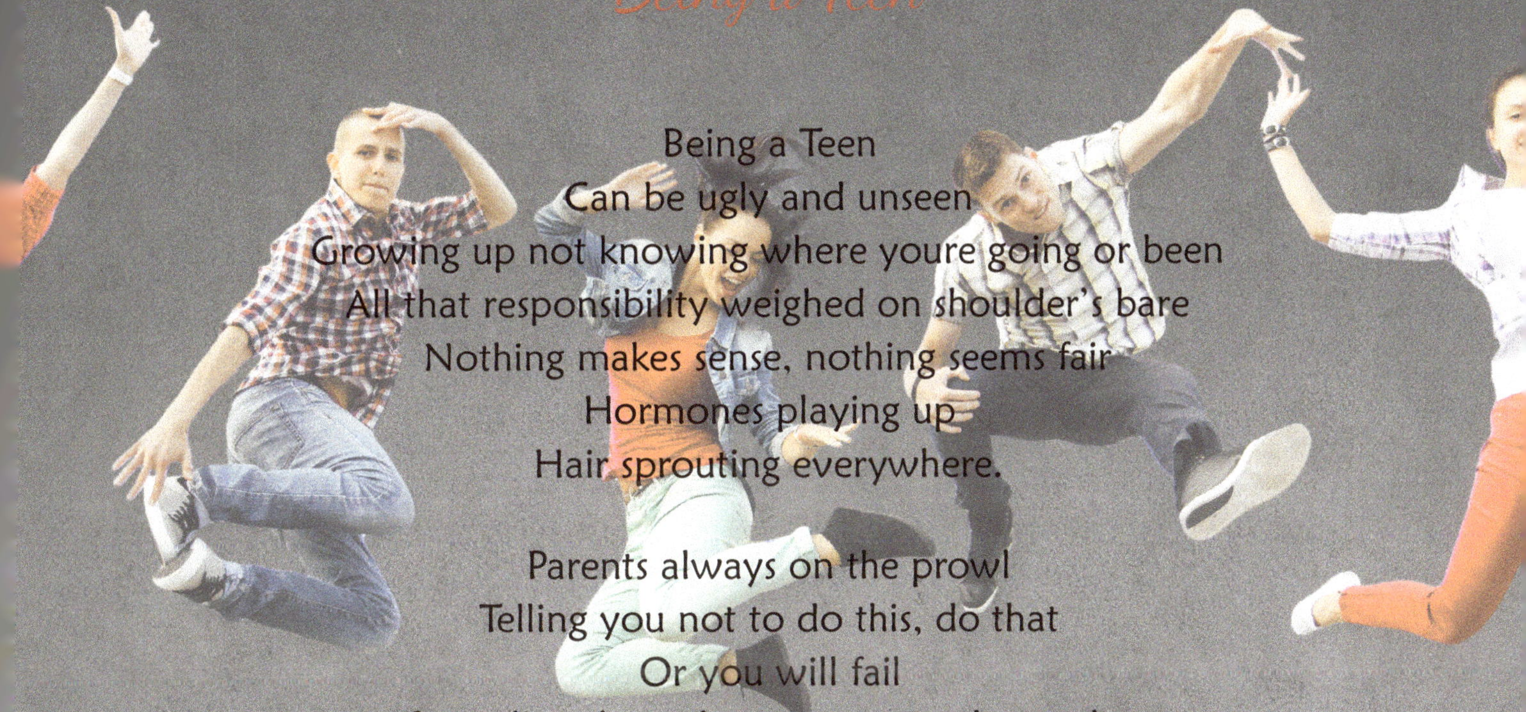

Being a Teen
Can be ugly and unseen
Growing up not knowing where youre going or been
All that responsibility weighed on shoulder's bare
Nothing makes sense, nothing seems fair
Hormones playing up
Hair sprouting everywhere.

Parents always on the prowl
Telling you not to do this, do that
Or you will fail
Struggling through exams to get the grades
Losing virginity and getting laid.

Leaving school to enter the world unknown
Leaving your parents, leaving home
Making your own way and having your own say
Making mistakes along the way.

Entering adulthood with promise and purpose
Adding value where others have lost
Feeling the pressure and trying not to worry
Working hard and having pleasure.

Is that what it's like to be a teenager
Or am I just a Lone Ranger?

School

School can be tough
Like growing up
Life can be rough.

All that discipline
Timetables and rules
Getting up and going to school
Being bullied and bearing the pain
Keeping silent and worried it will happen again.

Teachers can also be such a bore
Like many subjects you just want to ignore
Sitting exams can be such a chore
Late nights, burning the candle
Eyes getting tired, eyes getting sore.

Making friends is what it's all about
Kissing like lovers behind the bicycle sheds
Passing messages under the desks
Making fun of the teacher's pet.

Then oh what relief when the final bell is rung
Off we go to have some fun.

University

University can be so much fun
Lots to do but little study done
Parties somewhere every night
Go to bed when it gets light.

Get up at noon, far too soon
Stagger around aimlessly
In the nude
Finding clothes on the floor
Shed there probably the night before
Rubbing sleep out of eyes
As get hurriedly dressed
And head for University.

Breakfast eaten on the way out
To get to lectures before it's too late
Lectures over
Time for a break
Off to the refectory
To meet one's mates.

After a chin wag and a laugh
Then back to the campus for a bath
Refreshed and dressed in what one can find
Off to the bar
To down a few drafts.

As terms fly by and years pass by
Exams get closer
And studying gets harder
Days get longer
Whilst time in the bar gets shorter.

Such a relief when exams are over
And Graduation is such an honour and a pleasure
Then the next challenge to be faced
Getting a job
And joining the Rat Race.

The Meaning of Marriage

The more you have to go through
To be married to the one you love
Makes it all the more worthwhile
So simply do what your heart tells you to do.

If you keep working at it
The more wonderful it will be
Enjoying love and being together
For the rest of your lives
Don't wait, go seek and see.

So, take what life can give you
Double it, as there are no limits
For true love has no bounds
Take the leap of faith
And enjoy now and forever
What your hearts have truly found.

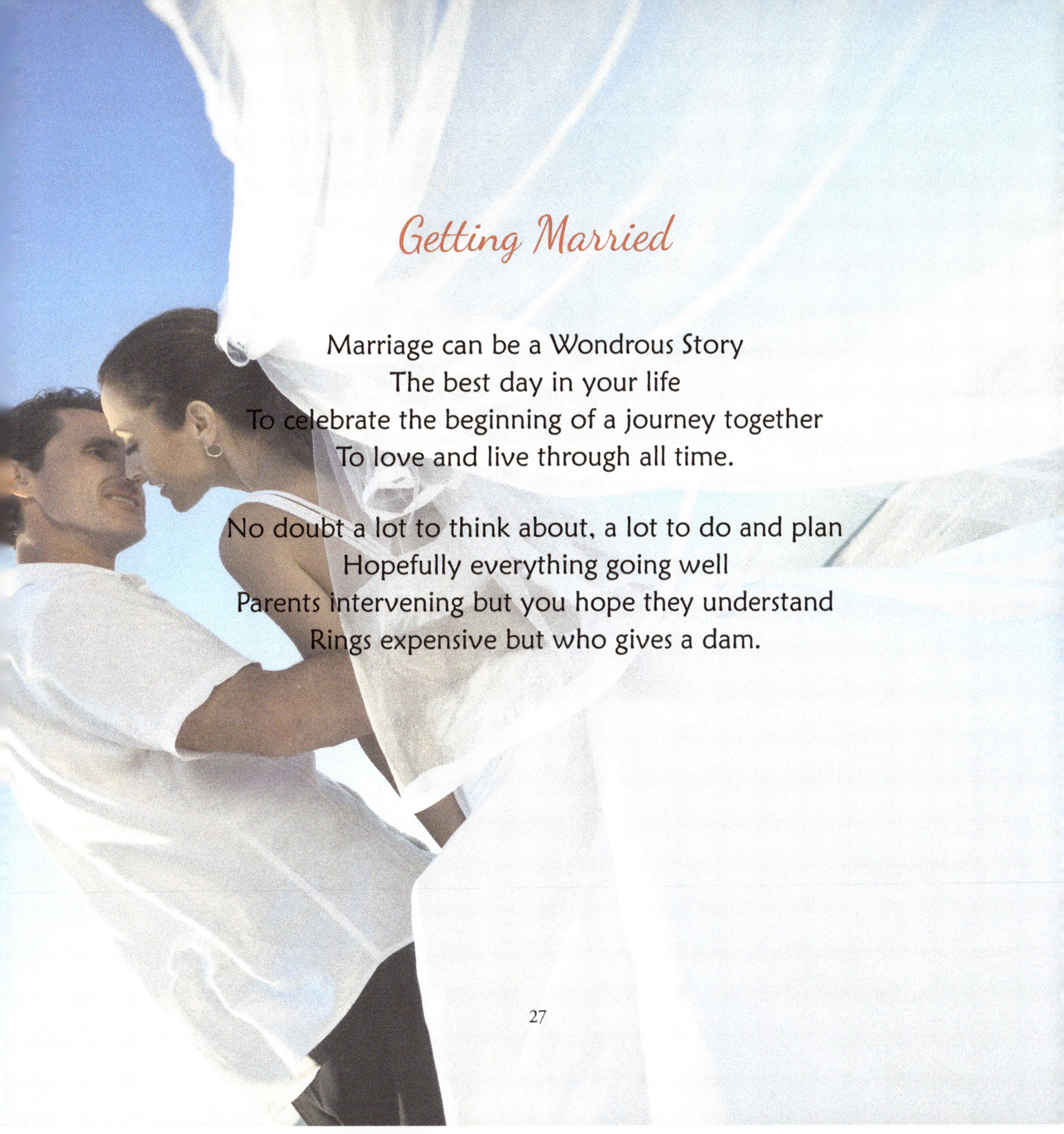

Getting Married

Marriage can be a Wondrous Story
The best day in your life
To celebrate the beginning of a journey together
To love and live through all time.

No doubt a lot to think about, a lot to do and plan
Hopefully everything going well
Parents intervening but you hope they understand
Rings expensive but who gives a dam.

Frocks and Bridesmaids a joy and a delight
Bridegroom never there when you want him
Except when creating havoc on stag night,
But duty bound, he turns up on the day with ring in hand
Supports you while you're waiting there
At the Altar nervous, shaking, with sweaty hands.

At the altar thinking will she come ?
Then Church bells rise to greet her in her white wedding gown
Heads turning as she glides down the aisle
Heart misses a beat, as she looks at you through the veil
That knowing look, that loving smile.

At the Altar, lost for words
Will I get it right?
Let's get it over with
Go out and enjoy the night.

Then everything happens so quickly
Everything goes right
People are joyful. dancing
Well into the night.

Until at least
The bride and groom leave
To start a new life
Never looking back
Only the future to embrace.

Living life to the full
Supporting and understanding each other
Sharing love, no matter the time or place
Living for each other
Eternal love divine.

Work—at the Zoo

I am up, so are you
And I'm off to work
In a building next to the zoo.

Monkeys play Ape for a grape
Chimps and Guerrillas too
So much for what goes on at work
Hope it's better in the zoo.

Hope life is better for you
Armed with a bucket and spade in hand
And plenty of sand
I'm stuck here with nowhere else to go.
I just want to be with you.

Old Age

Old Age creeps up upon you
faster than you think
Don't close your eyes or even blink
You don't realise you're getting old
Many feel younger
Until you get told.

Signs of old age start to appear
A wrinkle here, a wrinkle there
Can't bend over
Or run a Mile
Getting slower
But still wearing a smile
Don't do the things one used to.

Death—A New Beginning

Raise my soul from its earthly confine
To a place of solitude and heavenly divine
In a place where peace and love prevail
Where the world unites in a Universe thats parallel.

Where conscience is bared and re-borne
Goodwill and friendship shared and sworn
Where tranquillity and harmony know no bounds
Life departed but moving forward in ways we will never understand.

Ode to Gordon

However dark the night and grey the dawn
there will always be a light that shines
for Gordon the "man of heart"
for whom we mourn this day.

Ode to Ian

Ian, a close friend, talented business partner
Full of cheer, occasionally holding a beer
Sorely missed, and never drowned
He conducted himself with dignity, sense and pride
A true friend to me and those he found
Full of joy a plenty
Always up for life
Irrespective of any problem or strife.

Straight, would never bend
Whatever problem came his way
He was strong, always there to protect and defend
A true soldier, committed and blue
I miss him, as I'm sure will you.

I spent nine memorable years with Ian
Did many Visa runs from Saudi and had great fun!
Cairo, Addis Ababa, Beirut, Dubai, Bahrain to name some
We had a plan to buy a restaurant and bar
Somewhere distant, somewhere afar
Where all our friends and family could come
This I promise Ian
I will make it happen and dedicate it to you.

Life's Pitfalls

When Dark Descends

When dark descends and I can't take it
Hanging on, and just can't fake it
Am I dying or just crying?
Are you real or just lying?
Were you ever there for me?
Is my life lost to a desert of sands and storms at sea?
Am I wasted, life gone, lost and forlorn?
Sometimes wishing that I'd never been born!

And who are you to comment on my life and
demand I do this and do that?
Decide what I do as if I don't know what I'm doing
Giving me a load of crap
While I work and slave away
And you grunt and grow old and fat!

Loneliness

I sit in a lonely place in a cold dark cavern lost in time
Hollow, deep, black, bleak and sublime
Cold unfeeling lonely, only me, and nothing but mine.
Somehow seemingly unwanted desolate and unkind
That's what I think about me and mankind
At work others selling souls for a nickel and a dime
Never giving, always taking of me and mine
Lost in an endless fickle funnel of hate and crime.
In the dark, walking with ghosts in my shadows
Just me a lonely lovelorn figure
Hopeless, beaten and feeling unwanted
Awaiting love and warmth
With no finger on the trigger.

Hell

In the cold and darkness
Nowhere to turn
Every door closed
Only trap doors to hell can be found.
No light in the sky
Only burning fires down below
As the darkness descends
Taking our bodies and souls.

No Angels anywhere to be seen
No Knights in shining armour to be seen
Only death around the corner
Awaiting the cold call
Hell, hath no fury but
I hear it clearly
"Death to us all".

Hell in a Cell

Beware
As the Vultures soar overhead
In ever decreasing circles
They descend on the dead
As warm blood turns to cold
As bodies go stiff.

As souls leave their bodies
They feed on the rest.

We leave our bodies
And if nowhere to go
We will be trapped
Surely in hell.

Choking in a cell
Stinking and foul
Stuck down a well
Drinking our spit
Where we urinate and fell.

Ain't no life down here
Living dead everywhere.
Full of despair.
Heh, while its time
Turn around your life
For the good not the bad
Hell, just don't go there.

Solicitors

There is a firm of solicitors in Leeds
Unprofessional, unreasonable and unethical
Makes your heart bleed
They'll persist to abuse you
Bleed and freeze you cold dry.

Big Brotherhood in the sky
It really wants to make you cry
Talking crap, nonsense and full of shit
God knows how they get away with it.

Extortion, fancy suits and fees
Be alert, be aware
They are hell bound
To bring you to your knees.

The Witches Curse has been Cast

She has thrown the dice for the very last time

Trying to snatch my last nickel and dime

But the table is bare

And everyone has left

The place is deserted

There is no-one there.

She sits in her own cesspit and pool of despair

Even the Vultures (solicitors) have left

They don't care

They fly to feast another day

On yet another defenseless carrion of prey.

She sits in splendid isolation

Lonely and bereft

Awaiting the coffin and the kiss of death.

Ladies of the Night

Hanging round in sleazy bars
Flaunting sexy bras, tattoos and scars
Mauve varnish splashed on fingernails and toes
Keeping men's luggage labels as mere mementos
Brazen hussy, hooking men by the score
Nothing surprises me anymore.

Dealing with A Problem

A problem here, panic there
What shall I do?
Keep an open mind
Find the facts
Establish what is true.

Take a moment
Think it through
Don't be afraid
Do what is right
And take it one day at a time.

If you hit a snag, don't give up
Don't let it get you down
Take each challenge as it comes
Smile, deal with it and simply move on.

Disasters

An Earthquake

A distant rumble, a tiny tremor
Turning suddenly into a shockwave
of fear and horror.

The rumble grows louder and becomes a grumble
A table rocks, pots start shaking, plates tumble
The light above sparks, starts swinging and swaying.

The cupboard wavers, then comes crashing
Doors twist and scream on their hinges, then start swinging and banging
Windows start popping and glass everywhere shattering.

The world seems like it's coming to an end
The smell of fear and death already lurks and
lingers in the smoke-filled air.
Seems nowhere to go except a dead end
Nowhere to hide, nowhere to defend.

It's all too much to bear
As chaos reigns amidst the fear
And time seems endless
As the earthquake unfolds
And takes with it its deadly toll.

And as the bowels of the earth rip open
and take us
We stand amidst the dawning chorus of indomitable chaos.

Rooted in time while the world erupts
Dismissing us one by one
Then in waves tries to take us all
And say goodbye.

Yet for those that are left
Steadfast but bereft and bare
We stand alone with arms outstretched
Knees bending and trembling
Feet sliding and losing grip on the floor that is unerringly tilting
Is it time to pray or run the hell out of there?
Well, animal instincts come to bear.

The cats bolt on all fours through the nearest door
We follow in pursuit
Down flights of stairs
And in less than a heartbeat
We cross the hall
And fall into a crowded, confused street.

The street is moving violently under our feet
We're staggering like drunks you don't want to meet

Everything around is shifting and falling
Kids are screaming, women crying
It all seems very surreal and bewildering.

Then all of a sudden it stops
Total silence you could hear a pin drop!

Except for the rolling rumble of rubble as it
trickles down to settle in billowing clouds of dust.

People sitting on the floor
Looking aghast, looking lost
Like ghosts of the past, it freaks you out
Not knowing what to do
Just waiting silently, with nervous anxiety
For the next hell to break.
It's inevitable,
There's another quake on its way
Rumbling along
To take us away.

St James Bible Mark 13:8

For nation shall rise against nation, and kingdom against kingdom: and there shall be earthquakes in diverse places, and there shall be famines and troubles: these [are] the beginnings of sorrows.

Quran Chapter 22 Verses 1&2

1. O mankind! Fear your Lord and be dutiful to Him! Verily, the earthquake of the Hour (of Judgement) is a terrible thing.

2. The Day you shall see it, every nursing mother will forget her nursling, and every pregnant one will drop her load, and you shall see mankind as in a drunken state, yet they will not be drunken, but severe will be the Torment of Allâh.

A Hurricane is Coming

Born on the wind of a terrifying nightmare
Thundering by and shattering the sky
Destroying everything it can take
Leaving devastation in its wake.

Hurricane David
(Dominica, W. Indies, 1979)

A personal true story but one many will have experienced.

Early dawn
Not much sleep as we await our fate
Listening to the radio
For any news
Of the flight of a hurricane
That lies in our wake.

Hurricane passing us to the South
Then turned its eye north towards our island
Local Radio Station went off the air
Only 2 hours' notice to get to safety
In the confines of a hurricane proof shelter
Not been used for years.

So off we go to L Rose & Co
A mansion set in an unspoilt estate of pristine palm trees
Deep down, nested in the valley below
That's where we are heading
Fate unknown.

We arrive at 7.30 am
3 couples, our 2 dogs and the resident's cat
In the kitchen having a rum and coke or mebbe a beer and a chat
Locked in, a sense of excitement, as well as fear.

Outside, flocks of birds take flight
As winds rise, trees start to sway
Animals lie down, seemingly calm, sitting tight.

The noise becomes deafening
Doors and shutters rattle
We stand firm in the kitchen
Ready and waiting for the ensuing battle.

No-one moving,
Mebbe a slight tinkle and tremble
of a glass as the rum goes down
Welcome relief when faced with danger
No-one knows what's coming
But a sense of comfort
We are not alone
We are all together.

Then a vast rumbling noise
Followed by a whooshing sound
Bolts popping, tin screaming,
It's a hell of a din
As the roof lifts off.
Glasses shaking
But we are still stood firm on the ground.

Utensils, pots and pans sucked up into the void
Spinning, swirling within a tornado
Rising up then suddenly gone
And disappearing.

As if in a warp drive
Here one moment, then zapped into the air
Ain't no Fairground, more a melee in a Merry-go-round .
Did I see Dorothy in the Wizard of Oz fly by?
In a house flying across the sky?
Unfortunately, no this is not a film
It's real, threatening and frightening
We're facing death on this cold chilling morn.

No time to contemplate or live in a dream
This is a nightmare, the worst I've seen
Time to run, move on
So off we go
And rush into another room.

We evacuate to the lounge
We lock the door
And crouch behind on the polished floor
But the door starts to creak, buckle and bend
We shove antique furniture against it
But can see light emerging through the hinges and frame
So, without thought or feelings of shame
And nothing but ourselves to defend
We start breaking the legs off the furniture
And nail them to the moving door and buckled frame.

Lounge roof then lifts off, along with the door
We run to the back of the house to a small bedroom
And wait huddled, quiet, listening for more.

We place the cat on top of the wardrobe
While the dogs sit expectantly and like us retain a constant stare
At the cat and the roof, hoping they won't disappear.

Well not to be disappointed
Off they go, the roof and door, to join their friends
I sit a Merry-go-Round or Hell in a Den.

The wardrobe stands, but rocking and swinging with the cat
Gripping tightly with its claws as if death is waiting at the door
I tell my friends to leave as I try rescue him
But then, clutching the cat, rafters fall driving us both to the floor.

Friends return and provide a welcome hand
I'm rattled and stirred, cat is petrified
But glad to still be around
Limbs not broken just our pride as dust and rum clears from my head
And the cat is happy with feet back firmly on the ground.

We go to the balcony
Which has wire netting all around
And surround ourselves with tables and mattresses
And anything within reach
That will keep us safe and sound.

Then the nightmare returns
The evil wind whips up again
And peels back the balcony roof like a banana
That is stripped, yellow and bears no shame.

We dive over the balcony
Like mariners deserting a sinking ship
Bottle and animals in hand
We crawl underneath.

Then total silence
No sound outside.

Taking breath
We emerge into the open air
Now surrounded by a circulating white wall of death
I look up into the funnel towards the sky
Clear blue, and yet seemingly passing us by.
We are in the Eye.

In the Eye of the Storm
Surreal and temporarily safe
But it's moving slowly towards us
Across the estate
I realise it will hit us again
But from the other direction
At no stopping this one
To hell we are bound.

So back we go
Reinforce the cramped space that we know
To sit it out under the balcony
With determination and resolve.

Come hell and high water
And the persistent wind and rain
We survived it once
We will survive it again.

When it's all over
The sun again shines
Life returns to normal
And everything is just fine.

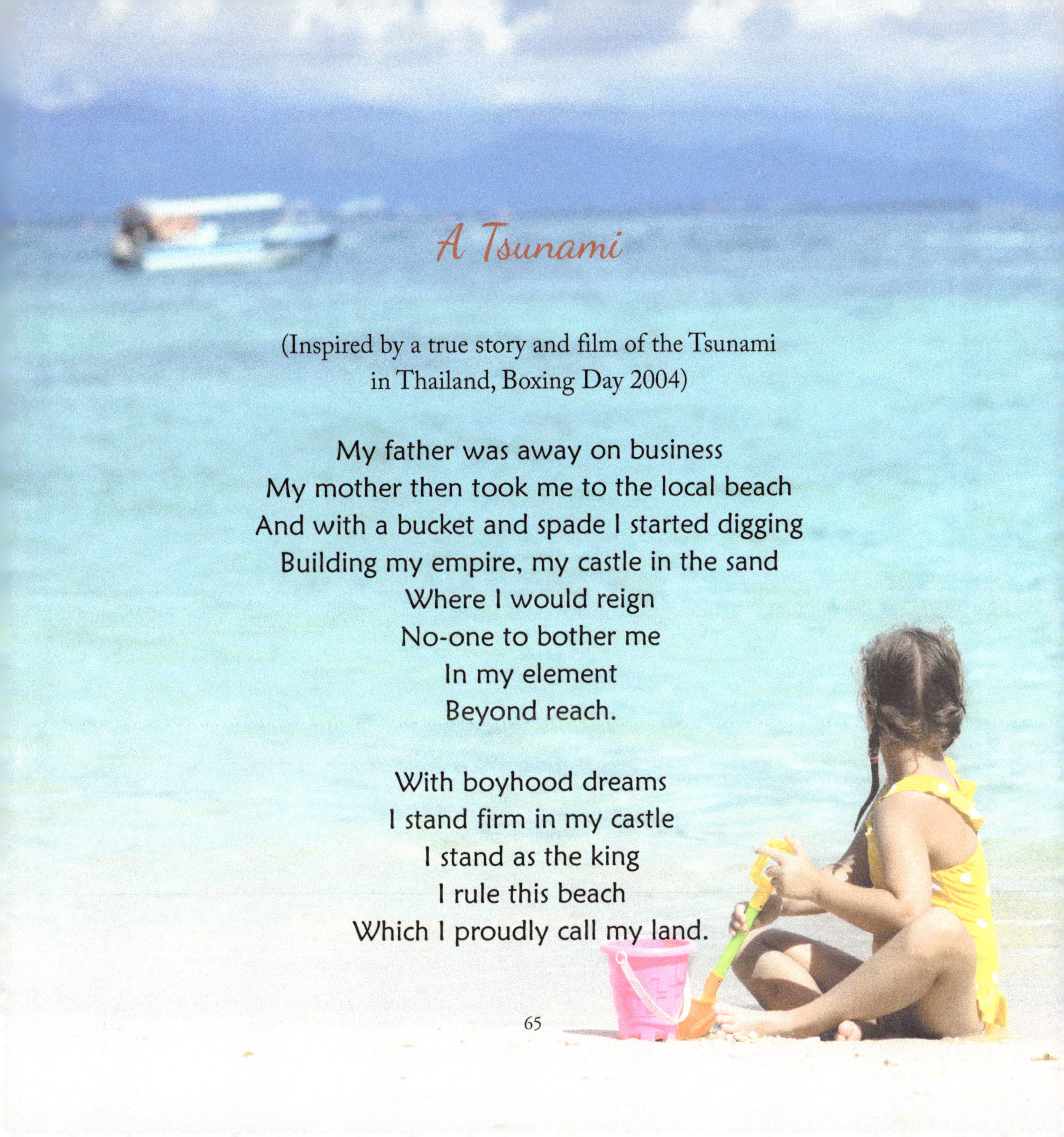

A Tsunami

(Inspired by a true story and film of the Tsunami
in Thailand, Boxing Day 2004)

My father was away on business
My mother then took me to the local beach
And with a bucket and spade I started digging
Building my empire, my castle in the sand
Where I would reign
No-one to bother me
In my element
Beyond reach.

With boyhood dreams
I stand firm in my castle
I stand as the king
I rule this beach
Which I proudly call my land.

As waters break
And spread their long fingers across the shore
I gather water in my little bucket
Take it back to my castle to mix with sand.
With spade in hand, I work hard to mix
And make a tower
Standing so high
Ever so grand.

High and mighty
Will my castle be
Made of pure gold
It will stand forever
Just wait and see !

So, I carry on digging a trench
To protect my castle with a moat
That will surround and protect me forever
All my loyal prospects for me to praise and gloat.
But my journey now seems ever longer to the sea
How can this happen, what can this be?
To collect much needed water
For my moat and me?

And as my beach gets longer
I need a bigger moat
To ward off intruders and strangers
That look at me strangely
But want to be just like me.

Also, strangely, the sea continues to recede
Reminds me of my dad's hairline
Surely it can't be
But who knows?
I'm confused mebbe?

So, the sea still continues to recede
Toward the distant horizon and shore
Am I seeing things?
I'm not sure.

People keep walking
Towards the water
Towards that distant shore
But it isn't there, is it?
I can't see it anymore.

People keep walking
But don't seem to get there.

Heh, I ain't just a kid
Ain't got anything to hide
I'm walking on the bright side
Ain't no kidding
I'm a king still ruling the tide .

Wow, my empire is expanding!
But now no water to fill my moat
Ok, I must improvise
I don't need a moat
Not even a boat.

But just a bigger trench and mebbe a fence
Mebbe I'm confused again
But I mean no offence.
I'm just a kid
Having fun.

So again, I start digging to me heart's content
Till I hear people shouting and running
I know not what for
I ignore them and carry on
Digging the trench, as before.

I keep digging
Till I can't see the top of the trench no more
All gone dark and quiet
I wonder why?

So, I scramble up
Look up and over, beyond my fortress and trench
But I can't see the sun
Then I see a wall of water as high as the sky
I realise, heh
I don't have to go get any more water, any more
My job is done.

Yes, yes , It's coming
The water is coming to me
To fill my trench
I've been waiting for so long
It will make me a king
But it's so big
Smothering and blotting out everything.
Oh my God, that includes me !

Then I hear my mummy shouting for me
Sounding an alarm
I climb out of my trench and wave
She screams
And runs towards me with outstretched arms
I panic and do the same
She tells me we are in danger
Must run and hide
To keep safe
And keep out of harm.

I say what about my castle ?
Looks at me like I'm stupid
Grabs my hand
We turn
My feet leave the ground
We take off and fly
We reach the promenade
No-one to be seen
No passers-by.

We run across the road to a hotel
But all the doors are locked
Nowhere to hide
Nowhere to turn it seems
But face the oncoming tide.

We run behind the hotel
And find a tall palm tree
Up you go she shouts
Just trust me she says
Just believe me !

Her hands round my waist
Her head up my bum
I gingerly move skywards
No clue what's going on.
Am I stupid or she just blind ?

I hold tight
As mum keeps pushing ever upwards
Where is she looking?
Is there no end in sight?

I hit my head on the roof of prickly palm fonds
And what seemed like coconut shies
Hang on–I hear my mother cry
As she straps me to the tree stump with her belt
And encircles my waist with her thighs
Can it get worse than this ?
I'm terrified.

Then the World falls in
Something hit me in the face
No idea what it can be
But hanging on it seemed forever
Just my mum and me.
I can't see or breathe
Life as I know it
I feel it's gradually leaving me.

I feel my arms and legs go limp
As I desperately cling to the tree
Held by my mum's belt and her knobbly knees
Frightened and glued to the tree
As painful as it can be
I close my eyes and pray
As mum had always told me.
Tried to reach out to her with no avail
As objects swirled past me and around me
I eventually lost consciousness
And fell to the ground.

I woke up at the bottom of the tree
Mum nowhere to be seen
Until I looked up
She was still clinging high up in the tree.

I called out and told her to come down
But she ain't moving
And I can't hear a sound.
I yelled out for help
Then a young man came
He was bleeding from head to foot
He looked up and without saying anything
Climbed up and helped her down.

Water was still swirling around my feet
The young man said we were still in danger
And should seek higher ground.

We return to the front of the hotel
Devastation everywhere
Windows shattered
No-one to be found.

We walk inside
Bodies floating
Bobbing, bubbling
But no other sound.

My mother closed my eyes and held me close
We ascended the stairs to the first floor
Then onwards, upwards to the roof
To the welcome of a breeze
And the welcome of the sun's glare
No surprise–no-one there!

I cried and my mother took me in her arms
and comforted me
I saw her look to heaven
And with silent lips
She looked away
And whispered a prayer
To heaven, and for me.

I calmed in my mother's arms
I opened my eyes
Everything around
Stripped barren and bare
But I was ok
She was with me
She was there.

Then the young man shouted looking inland
Waters returning with force
Bringing back everything it had gathered
Scattered then found.

We stood there rooted in trepidation and fear
Nothing like it I had ever seen
And hopefully will never see again
Here or elsewhere
Standing rooted in fear and total silence...

The water came back at us like a battering ram
Like it was seeking vengeance and rooting us out
But then stopping, then encircling
And passing us around
Returning to the sea

Now spent
Returning calmly from whence it came
Not to be traced, sought or found.
So...
We sat in silence
For what seemed an hour
Everything quiet, surreal
Feeling unsafe and unsure
Not sure if we were alive
Or safe or sound.

Nothing moving on the empty beach and shore
Tired, exhausted, beaten, bruised and sore
Constantly bleeding from all pores.

We sat there unmoving
Scratched and forlorn
All lost, all gone
Never the same
Many loved ones lost
Never to be seen again
They're gone

Never returning
Buried at Sea
That's for sure.

My mother washed and wrapped bandages
Around the brave young man, his name unknown
Truly a saint and a saviour
Hardly making a sound
But truly a man on a mission
Duty bound.

In the morning my mother awoke
The young man nowhere to be found
Gone to rescue other survivors no doubt
In the baren wasteland that now surrounds
Then never seen again as he journeys far
Seeking and saving lost souls
A destiny, in lands that have no bounds.
We gathered ourselves with resolve and renewed vigour
Went to find our house, which we eventually found
Under rubble, nothing left
But memories littered on the ground.

People like ghosts
Covered in mud
Emerging from nowhere
Staggering around
Yet giving us water, comfort and first aid
Then in a jeep to a hospital to be checked
Then a shelter, safe and sound

Years later, we rebuilt
Father had returned
Gave us strength
Strength we felt we never had before or found.
But we never gave up
Onwards and upwards we went
Rebuilding day by day
A community joined
By love, duty, honour and respect
In total harmony.

Yes, we moved on
Never forgetting our soul and our roots
Never forgetting what we had been through
Never forgetting what we had seen.
Never forgetting where we had been.

Monsoon

They come frequently
Like the rising moon
They form and grow in force
Like nothing seen before.

They rise and grow
From the ocean's floor
Rising up to darken the sky
As they encroach and threaten
Unprotected shores.

Causing havoc and destruction
In their wake
As they cross the land
Heavens divide
Some people sleep
Whilst others awake
Aware
And running for higher ground.

Cries for help
Can be heard
From treetops and rooftops
As they bend
But can't defend
Against a relentless unforgiving flood.

As the deluge of rain and flood
Continue to ravage the land
People lost, never found.

Bobbing heads passing by
In the torrent of water
Raking the ground
Carrying everything before it
Including the dead.

Flood surging
Bringing misery and despair
Mixed with blood and mud
Running wild everywhere.

Sweeping away villages and life
Destroyed in a single wave
Leaving bereft
A barren empty land.

Only the sound of silence
Can now be heard
Broken only by prayers of hope
Until the next Monsoon comes
Bringing death and misery
Once again.

Ice Wind- A Journey Too Far

Yes the greatest challenge I have ever faced
Starting a mile behind the start of the race
A pack of wild dogs baying and fighting amok
Loosely roped to a sleigh of wood that has rot
Where I stand uneasy swaying in the bitter cold
Saliva freezing on my shabby clothes
Waiting but raring to go
Waiting for you
For God's sake,
Come, let's go.

The journey ahead is a difficult one
Fraught with danger
Fear-and-some
Nowhere to shelter
Nowhere to hide
Difficult to navigate
Sometimes difficult to find
Just you and me
And a wolf pack makes three
Baring our teeth and bearing on.

Hail biting deep in our lungs
Hoarse breath making for an earie song
Eyes bulging in their sockets
Running red in the frost
Hands frozen,
Numb, not moving
Seemingly lost.

Mouth grimaced
Clamped tight
Against the wind
In this cold dark night
Which we can't defend or fight
Through the rugged ice-storm we hunch and bunch
Losing sight of each other as we trudge and crunch
Through drifting banks of snow
Engulfing us and not letting us go
Wondering if we will make it to the journey's end
Fighting for breath and life as we turn the next bend.

Tearing us apart
Wearing down our soul
Weakening our resolve
It's time to go.

All alone in the wilderness
Our senses on alert
Wind whistling around us
Death is a cert.

Asteroid

A speckle of dust passing almost unseen in time and space
Grows unknowingly into a threat that we must all face
Like a falling star illuminating the night sky
The Asteroid appears to aimlessly wander by
But descending towards Earth
And getting ever so near
It explodes in a shower of light
as it enters the atmosphere.

Gaining velocity as it comes closer
Blotting out the sun as it gets ever so nearer
A boulder as big as a mountain that seems to get bigger and bigger
Then a mighty crash that sounds like thunder
As it ploughs into the Earth and leaves everything asunder
Creating shock waves that encircle the earth
Flattening everything in its girth.

Clouds of dust mushrooming
Darkening the sky
Drastically changing the climate as days go by
And as a cold cruel polar winter descends
Everything perishes
Everything must come to an end.

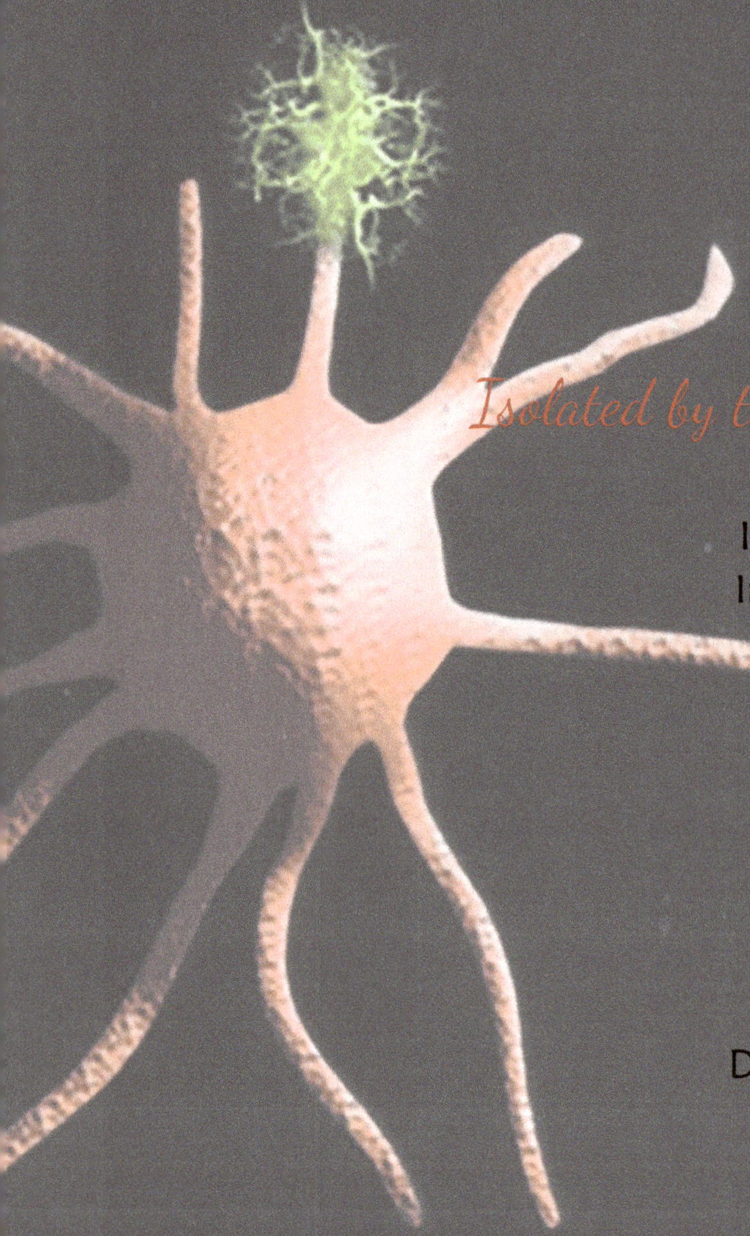

Covid 19

Isolated by the Virus or is it Dementia?

Isolated by the virus again
In the middle of the desert
Mental, going insane
Or is it dementia?
Who knows?
Someone remind me.

So true
Life in prison isn't so bad
Nor is being mental
Dementia also doesn't help
and today
Whatever day it is
I hope can find my way
To be tested at the hospital.

To be tested, then rested
Bored, no-one to talk to
Nothing to do
I hope I don't test positive
I hope it doesn't happen to others
Especially to you.

I promise I will keep you posted
After I've been tested.
But I can't seem to remember

Who the hell are you?
Well there's the proof !

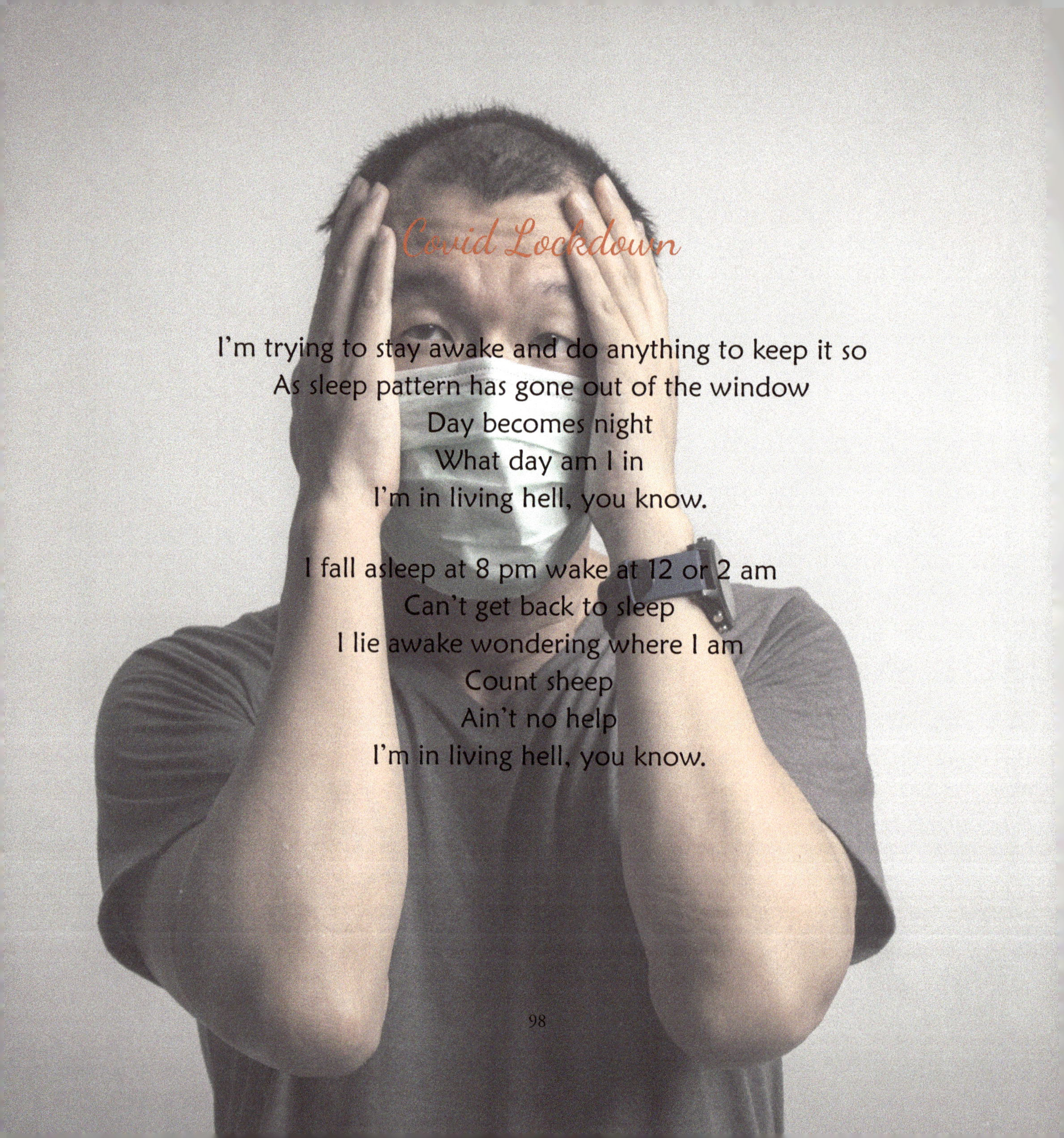

Covid Lockdown

I'm trying to stay awake and do anything to keep it so
As sleep pattern has gone out of the window
Day becomes night
What day am I in
I'm in living hell, you know.

I fall asleep at 8 pm wake at 12 or 2 am
Can't get back to sleep
I lie awake wondering where I am
Count sheep
Ain't no help
I'm in living hell, you know.

No point lying there
Naked and bare
Nothing to do
But your body to view
No good films on TV
Nothing to see and do
Just ain't much to do
About anything.

Its 8pm I'm doing anything to stay awake
On your own, it's truly a heart ache
Do anything to get back to a normal life
So, I write this poem to pass the night
Simple, true but who gives a shite.

The Virus Hits

Yes, it's me on my own
Isolated not free
I believe I have the virus
But no-one wants to test me
I'm on the HS front line
But can't go in
No one there
No-one here
To care for me.

No family, no friends
Yes, it's only me
Credit running out
No communication
No job, no money, no food,
Only depressing Covid TV.

Temperature rising
Throat dry
Forever coughing
Can't think
I'm on the brink
Feel I'm dying.

Burning fever
Loss of function
Nothing working
I ain't healing
I'm dying
God save the Queen
God save me.

I'm in a coma
Somewhere strange
In a Unit
White and old
I hear voices talking
Giving me encouragement mebbe
I have to stay but wanna go
I have to survive
But I've lost my soul
Is there life out there?
I need to know?

Yes, I clearly hear them now
They say they are looking after me
But I'm in a coma
Am I dreaming?
Are they aliens?
Are they real?
And do they really care?
I don't know.
I now see a light at the end of a tunnel
Is it death or survival?
I do not know
But I'm on my way
I need to know
I'm just going there
On my way
I simply do nothing but pray.

I pray hanging onto vivid memories of the past
Hoping it was now
But am I here or gone tomorrow?

I look to faith but the chapels are empty
Where's the vicar
on video
Preaching to millions but no-ones listening
Whats the point
Life is empty.
It comes down to this
Live or die!
End the suffering, hoping to find bliss
Or fighting on through pain and griss !
Knowing there is still a life to lead
Giving, enjoying and making a difference
Is what I need.

Call the Angels to gather round you
Hear their wings on the wind of your prayers
Hear and embrace their songs and lullabies
To soothe you and guide you away from your
downward journey of despair.
Hear them whisper their undying love and care
Helping you recover, get strong and be able to bear
The future in your hands
With nothing to fear
With so much love, so much to share.

The future of mankind is in your hands
Not easy for many to understand
But if you set your mind
You can and will find it
Reach out and grab it
Convert it
Show care and kindness
And change all mankind.

Coming Out of Covid

Come together
Right now
Feel the energy
Harness the power.

Come alive
Come around
Life is now for living
As joy and love rebounds.

In isolation, uncertainty
Loved ones lost
Yet new hopes raised
New friends found.

There are no ghosts
They exist no more.
Feel the moment
Awaken your soul
Raise your spirit
Live your goals.

Breathe the air
Hear the sounds
Enjoy
Reach out
Look around.

Raise your hands
And touch the sky
Feel your feet
Leave the ground
Raise your spirit
Let it soar.

Take everything in
Forget what was lost before
As life rebounds
Opportunities galore
So much to live for
So much more to explore.

No need now for prayer
Just enjoy life
Live life
Like never before.

Revival Song

I walk where death prevails
It spits in your eye, begging you to die
With the many that have fallen before
To die in isolation and no-one there.

The virus, seemingly flying with wings,
Born on the souls of despair
Like an uncontrolled wind that holds no bounds
Searching, seeking, devouring every living soul
As it creeps upon you unknown, unfound
Across every shore, through every door
Silent but deadly, unspoken but sure.

Yet we stand before it
We will not relent
We are strong
And we'll master it.
Standing firm, hand on heart
Together yet lonely, mebbe apart
Notwithstanding, we are strong
Together, we make ready for it
To recover and make a new start.

With belief in our very soul
Goals high and sights afar
We are the living, not the dead
We will revive, we will survive
Nothing can stop us
We will rise up and again be strong, be alive.

I sense it in my soul
I feel it on the wind
I know we can do it
We will get better
We will get through this
To the very end.

The End is Nigh

A spec. of dust in the passage of time
What was a city is now levelled and benign
Armageddon arrived and finished it off
Everything destroyed, everything lost.

The World as we know it
Crumbling and in decline
Nothing exists, nothing survived
Surrounded by silence
Surreal and sublime.

Nations became wrathful, and our own wrath came
The ruining of the Earth, by mankind
Wars, famines, earthquakes, and epidemics of deadly disease
Descending endlessly upon us
Panic and chaos reigns.

It was bound to happen
Just a matter of time.

And at the appointed time
Will the unjust leaders, and the inglorious dead now be judged?
And will the slaves, the poor, the proph-
ets and holy ones fearing God's name
Inherit the Earth with all its shame?

The Coming of the End

The Earth will shake
Cities will lean and fall in their quake
Forests uproot and leave the ground
Rivers flood amok and spread tons of mud around
Volcanoes awake, fires alight
Causing havoc
Which has no bounds
As humans run, taking flight.

Heavens divide and clouds collide
Lightning strikes
As hurricanes and tornadoes thunder
Seas rise and roll
As tsunamis sweep the coastlines
And take their deathly toll
Leaving life in ruin
Shedding misery and asunder.

Leaving nothing in their quake
But death and destruction
Emptiness and turmoil
As we emerge confused and forlorn,
In the dawn of their wake.

All is Lost
God rest our Souls.

Where are the Leaders?

Where are the leaders?
High aloof in their liar
Safe from the truth
That no-one can bear.

Surely the buck must stop with us
As there's no-one else to trust
Just you me the dog and next doors cat
All sat on the same rugged mat
All pondering what will happen next.

So, who's going to get off the mat?
Doesn't matter so long as someone does
Doesn't matter if we make mistakes'
Life is for the living
Let's get what we can take.

The love of adventure
We will learn to change and adapt
Move upwards and onwards
Before it's too late
And the dog or the cat craps in our lap.

Black And White

Is it surprising?
Black can be good
While white can be bad.

Oh, let us all
Listen to music from our soul

And if we can listen
History tells us
What the truth beholds.

Unfortunately, we don't listen
We let and live a lie
In truth, its brutal, dark, distressing, cold and true
But all we see is beauty, gold and skies crystal clear and blue.

If we were all educated
How different it would be
For all of us
Yes, that includes everyone
And you and me.

Yet no-one seems to care
No-one's listening to the truth
Even though it's cold and laid bare
Yet it's there behind and before us
Social media blessed with sharing universal truth
For all to see
In black white, colour and sound
So why aren't governments serving the people ?
Why are they so slow to be duty bound ?

Really, ain't no missing what's going on
What's cruel and unforgiving
What's hitting the ground.

Knee pressed on my neck on the ground.
Ain't right, can't fight
When I'm cuffed and bound.

I try call for my Mother
Can't breathe
I'm fighting for my life
Can't reach her
Life has left me.

White supremacy, brutal black suppression and slavery
When will it end ?
Hopefully in this century.

It's so sad,
World biased
Has it gone mad?

In School we were not told the truth
Only that the White Man rules
Black people only told to die for dis country
Yet some still imprisoned in slavery and deprivation
Nowhere to turn but left to die in abject misery.

Where can they now turn?
Demonstrate to the bitter end?
Tear statues down?

Fury that knows no bounds?
Ultimate despair
And no justice to be found
Except discrimination and being pushed to the ground.

How can that be in a civilised society ?
But the prejudiced, the minority, the coloured, the poor
No-one to defend them
It's a cruel World
That's for sure.

Always in the front line
Ready to take the bullet and die.

Indoctrinated, they must fly the flag for a foreign country
Not for the World or their own country
Not even for all humanity.

Equal all, everyone?
When will we tell the truth ?

When will Brothers and Sisters across the World
Unite, live in harmony and peace

Love each other, live as one
Now and forever
One day, truly it will come.

No end to despair
But is it over now?
Let's hope that truth and humanity prevail
Let's all go there.

One and all, all in arms
Singing the song
Of love, no more harm
Reaching out with kindness and honesty
Touched with the warmth of our souls and our hearts

Bearing friendship and gifts
Love and understanding
Will have no bounds.

For all Mankind
Let's find a way
To another brighter day.

Let racism cease
Let us all rest in peace.

Brothers & Sisters in Arms

Much goes on in this World
Much we do not know
Only those that wield the power
Are clearly in the know.

What happened to religion, equality and democracy?
Or has the World just gone crazy ?
Are we not creative and caring human beings?
Or are we just bone idle and lazy?

When will we realise, we have a purpose
That we have been foretold
To live life to the full
To be forthright, honest and bold
So that we can fulfil our destiny for the benefit of all.
Brothers & Sisters join in arms
Brothers & Sisters join in peace
Where no-one will come to harm

No one will fall from grace.
Learning to love each other
With undying trust, fervent hope and lack of fear
Where we are all healers
All believers
Healing those in our care.

The Sound of Running Water

The sound of running water in a stream
For some never heard never seen
Nature flowing as in a dream
Never ending
Till it reaches the sea.

Pure and honest
Knows no bounds
Like life itself
It ebbs and flows.

Thus we must learn
Duty bound
To protect nature itself
As it protects us
Never ending
Living, breathing
Never drowned
There always to be found.

A river flowing to the sea
A sea of dreams
For you and me.

Fulfilling Destiny

"Do not let your Mind stop you from doing
what your Heart tells you to do".

Today, tomorrow and the days that follow
I will walk from the past
And do that which I should have done
Long ago.

To fulfil my destiny
Do that which is right
I will be bold and hold strong
Each step yielding truth
Shedding light.

Seeing, believing and knowing,
All will come True.

True or False

Sometimes everything seems black and white
Sometimes grey
But do you really know
What is right?

And when you walk from the darkness towards the light
You may be able to open your eyes to see the future
Is it bright?
Can you see what you've missed?
Was it ok or was it a fight?

So, trust your inner instinct
And forgive others if they don't know wrong from right

Don't beg steal or borrow,
It may only bring sorrow. to those that might.
Rise above the lies and deceit and turn the other cheek
See it from another angle
Without blame or remorse
Or even worse, revenge
Otherwise, there may be no tomorrow.

Whatever it is, look forward
Know what is right
Stick by your morals
Don't enter a fight
That no-ne can win.

Life is precious
Hold it tight
Smile, rise above
Make it fun
Share delight.

So, smile when things look bleak and down
When things get really black when you thought they were brown

Hide those bad thoughts, hold them down
Walk on water, you will not drown
Look to the sky, do not frown
Be bright, confident know your way
And let others follow, and make it your day.

The journey ahead may not always be clear
But if you open your eyes
Towards the truth and the light
You will be guided to push and make it
To things that are so dear.

And while the path may be rocky ahead
In the end you will get there
Believe me it's true
Nothing can stop you
Just lead and dont be bled
Your blood is blue
Its righteous, it's in the bible
There to be read.

My Angel

There is an Angel close to me
So close but she I cannot see
She guides me through life
But doesn't talk to me.

I know she is there
Bizarre it seems
Like she's nowhere
But I feel her around me
I can't explain
A guardian Angel
Looking over me.

But I can't depend on this
Though it gives me comfort and she is kind
But I must take the present and the sign
Move forward now and through time.
Yes time and life is endless
That I believe and what I leave behind will follow me through time
What I gain and what I experience travels with me always
As do others even if they don't know their path is the same as mine.
It's there to find

It will be fun
Just listen on the wind
Just open your mind.

Angels in my Arms

I laugh, I often cry
I don't know why
I'm lost in love
Leaving one who nearly destroyed me
To find another who abuses me
Time after time.

Whenever will I learn maybe never before I die
But I have a heart and an angel by my side
She is sat beside me now
Telling me I am moral and strong
I will live the future
Someday strong

Living happy contented and just fine.
Trapped in time,
Suppressed mebbe
But yes, I will be fine.

I know the angels are with me now
Laughing shouting my song
I know now I will not come to harm
As we will all be angels-in-arms sometime.

Let's Travel the World

Let's travel the World
Before it dies before our eyes
Let's make a difference
Help the World unite.

Let's do it
Before it's too late
Before nations are destroyed
In a perpetual fight
Against nature, the climate
and anything in sight.

Nations lacking morals and might
Governments in turmoil
Democracy in flight
It won't be easy
it will be a tough fight.

The answer is simple
It's down to the people
Intellectual leaders
Who see the light,
Who can save the planet?
Do what is right?

So let's rally around them
Do the simple things
Value life, nature
others and ourselves
It's now or never
So join the fight.

About the Author

Dave was born and grew up on the shores of England and following his schooling travelled around the World working for consultancies and institutions like PWC, the World Bank and United Nations, in some of the richest and indeed poorest places on the planet. Besides troubleshooting projects, sometimes in the middle of nowhere, sometimes left on his own, he learned much about people and life, its challenges and experiences, some deep and profound. His love of poetry grew overtime through experience of love, disasters and travel. He has also published the first book of a trilogy of love poems the first entitled "Illustrated Book of True Love Poems". For those experiencing love it is a must.

davecourtneyshore@gmail.com

"Those seeking an inspirational poetry collection for everyday reading will find that in this book's colorful pages."

—Nicole Yurcaba
The US Review of Books

Book of True Life Poems

by Dave Courtney-Shore

*"And whilst I am a Survivor
They are Warriors"*

This poetry collection ebbs and flows between life's cycles and experience's lessons. Readers travel through four sections: "The Journey of Life," "Life's Pitfalls," "Disasters," and "Life's Hopes." In each section, readers encounter familiar and unfamiliar paths that lead through childhood's fun times, adolescence's struggles, and adult life's labyrinth of complexities. While the poems primarily focus on life's ups and downs, poems discussing other issues challenging the world, such as inequality and climate change, receive a bit of the versified spotlight.

The US Review of Books

AUTHORS PRESS

CREATIVE BOOKS

The book's first section opens with "Birth—A New Beginning." This poem celebrates the "overwhelming, miraculous, stupendous" moment when a child enters the world. In the same section, readers encounter "Children of Destiny." This poem celebrates the often unseen and overlooked strength and resilience children possess that, if adults allowed them to, hold the power to transform and inspire older generations. In the spirit of Thomas Hood's "I Remember, I Remember," these poems cast a bright light that provides an exciting opening for readers. The collection's second section takes a more ominous turn. Pieces like "When Dark Descends" address the overwhelming weight that hopelessness places upon the bearer. Similarly, the poem "Dealing with A Problem" poses solutions for handling conflict and adversity and offers hopeful solutions for seemingly impossible circumstances.

The third section guides readers through a multitude of ecological disasters. What makes this section a powerful one is its potential duality. Some readers may interpret the poems literally and as poetic commentary about climate change and the consequences of humanity's neglect and abuse of the natural world. Other readers, however, may approach this section more metaphorically, seeing the poems' natural imagery as symbolic and representative of the storms and disruptions permeating life. For example, readers can interpret "An Earthquake" as simply a portrayal of an earthquake or as a symbol of a destructive, life-changing event: "The rumble grows louder and becomes a grumble." Furthermore, the turbulent imagery in "Monsoon" echoes life's unpredictability: "Like the rising moon / They form and grow in force." Thus, poems based on personal experience such as "A Tsunami" reinforce that duality.

Despite the brunt force of "Disasters," which at times may leave readers wondering if humanity's mishaps can ever be corrected, readers eventually find themselves on the rhyming shores of "Life's Hopes." This final section houses poems like "Fulfilling Destiny," which reinforces the concept of personal pursuit and the contentment that comes with fulfilling one's purpose: "I will walk from the past / and do that which I should have done." Other poems like "Let's Travel the World," which boldly states "Before it dies before our eyes," encourage readers to seize their moments while addressing climate change's ever-looming threat.

A careful balancing act of life's positives and negatives, this collection bears the contemporary meditative and reflective spirit of Saundra T. Russell's *Apocalyptic 2020*. The collection's relevancy makes it a powerful read, especially for newcomers to the poetry genre. Other readers will appreciate its focus on personhood. Those seeking an inspirational poetry collection for everyday reading will find that in this book's colorful pages.

Book Reviewed by:

Nicole Yurcaba
The US Review of Books

CPSIA information can be obtained
at www.ICGtesting.com
Printed in the USA
LVHW070945080122
708050LV00032B/2503

9 781643 146942